Map of China

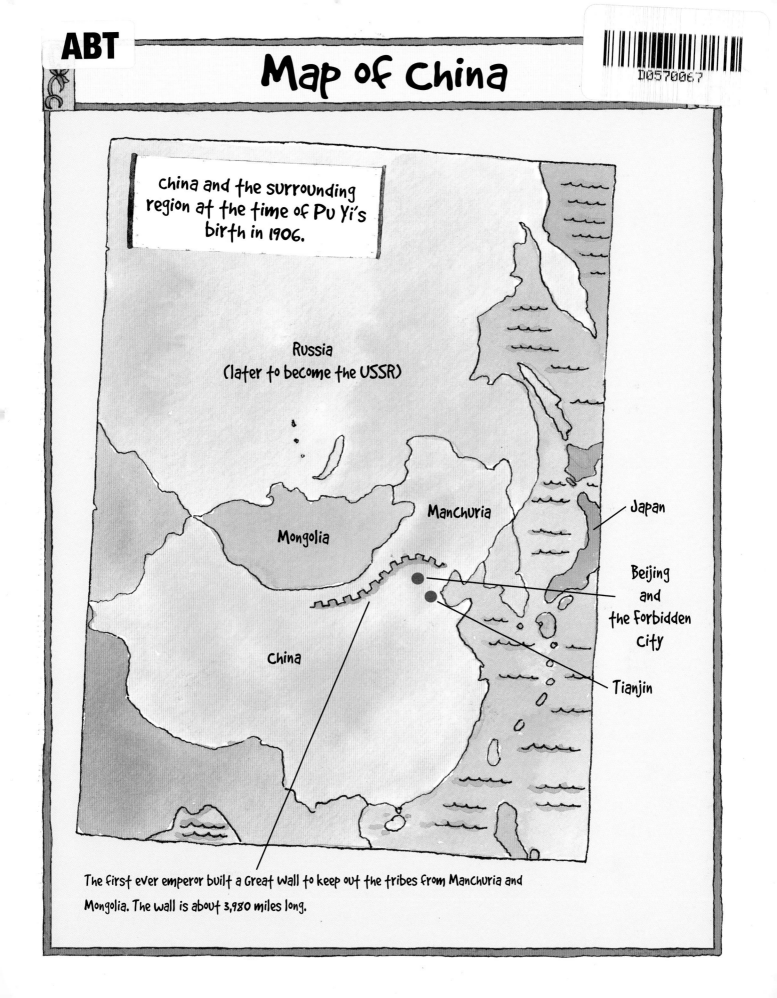

china and the surrounding region at the time of Pu Yi's birth in 1906.

Russia
(later to become the USSR)

Mongolia

Manchuria

Japan

Beijing and the forbidden City

Tianjin

China

The first ever emperor built a Great Wall to keep out the tribes from Manchuria and Mongolia. The wall is about 3,980 miles long.

 Children's Publishing

First published in Great Britain in 2003 by Brimax™
an imprint of Octopus Publishing Group Ltd
2-4 Heron Quays, London E14 4JP

Text and illustrations © Octopus Publishing Group Ltd 2003

This edition published in the United States of America in 2003 by
Peter Bedrick Books
an imprint of McGraw-Hill Children's Publishing,
a Division of The McGraw-Hill Companies
8787 Orion Place
Columbus, Ohio 43240-4027

www.MHkids.com

Library of Congress Cataloging-in-Publication Data is on file with the publisher.

© Octopus Publishing Group Ltd 2002

Printed in China.

1-57768-554-7

1 2 3 4 5 6 7 8 9 10 BRI 09 08 07 06 05 04 03 02

the last EMPEROR

By Jeremy Smith

Illustrated by Anthony Lewis

CONTENTS

PETER BEDRICK BOOKS
Columbus, Ohio

Birth of a Special Baby

On February 7th, 1906 a baby boy was born in **China** to a wealthy and privileged family. He was named Pu Yi and was destined to become an important historical figure. For nearly two thousand years China had been ruled by successive **dynasties** (families), each one headed by an **emperor**. Each dynasty ruled for a few centuries. Invasion by tribes from **Manchuria** and **Mongolia** was a constant threat. Eventually, though, the **Manchu** tribes took control of China. Pu Yi's family were Manchus and their **Qing dynasty** had been in power for over 250 years when Pu Yi was born. Manchu people considered themselves superior to Chinese people; they spoke a different language and wore a different style of clothing. The Manchu **imperial** family was very unpopular with its Chinese subjects.

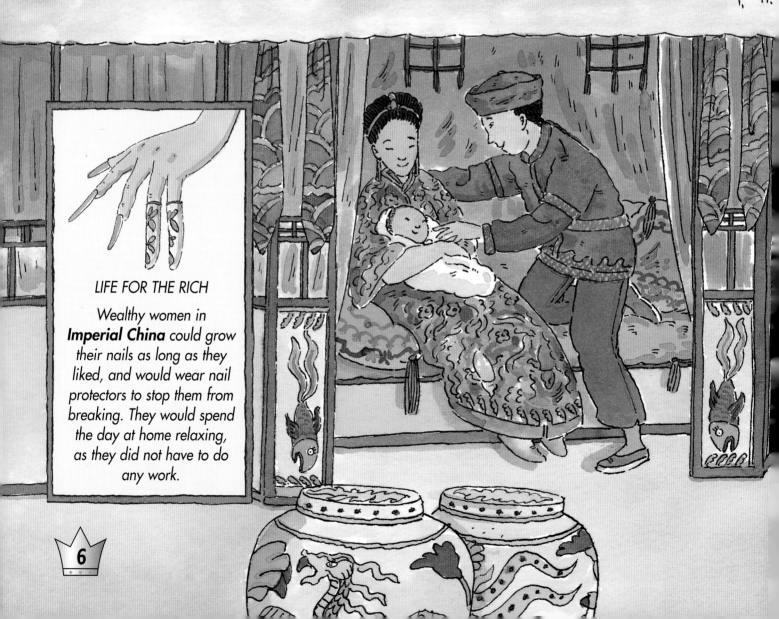

LIFE FOR THE RICH

*Wealthy women in **Imperial China** could grow their nails as long as they liked, and would wear nail protectors to stop them from breaking. They would spend the day at home relaxing, as they did not have to do any work.*

6

Poor people worked in the fields from sunrise until sunset. The countryside was mainly a place for the rich to live, so the poor were forced to live in dirty, polluted cities. Families were packed together in tiny houses, often with only one room. Sometimes they even had to share the house with their animals!

Pu Yi's family enjoyed a very comfortable lifestyle. They were served by many servants. As members of the ruling class, they lived in the countryside, in a house specially built to avoid evil spirits and ill winds. They spent a lot of money on beautiful jewelry and expensive clothes, and worked as little as possible. Although Pu Yi's father, **Prince Chun**, was the nephew of the ruler of China, the **Dowager Empress Cixi**, he only dabbled in politics. Instead, he spent most of his time going to parties. His powerful aunt had promised him, though, that if he produced a son, she would make sure that the child became the next emperor of China.

The forbidden City

When Pu Yi was almost three years old, he was taken from his family and smuggled into the **Forbidden City** in the dead of night. As promised, the tiny boy had been chosen by the Dowager Empress Cixi on her deathbed to be the next leader of China. Cixi was Pu Yi's great aunt, a fearsome woman nicknamed the "dragon lady." The Forbidden City was in **Beijing**, and was sealed off from the outside world by towering walls and a moat. Within the walls were many palaces, temples, and beautiful gardens built by past emperors. Commoners were not allowed inside the city. Only the imperial family, their servants, and advisors could enter.

Sedan chairs were a popular form of transportation for important officials and the rich. The emperor was carried around the Forbidden City in a jewel-studded sedan chair held by slaves. In later years, sedan chair races were held in many cities in China!

The Last of the Manchu Emperors

Daoguang Emperor
(reigned 1821-1850)
|
Xianfeng Emperor
(reigned 1851-1861)
married to Empress Cixi
(reigned as Dowager Empress
1862-1908)
|
Tongzhi Emperor
(reigned 1862-1874)
|
Guangxu Emperor
(reigned 1875-1908)
|
Emperor Pu Yi
(reigned 1908-abdicated 1912)
The Last Emperor

In China, women were not allowed to rule directly, so Cixi had become a **dowager empress**. This meant she could choose a weak emperor and still rule the country by bullying and controlling him from behind the scenes. She chose her young son to become the **Tongzhi Emperor** in 1862. Then, when he died, she made Pu Yi's sickly uncle the **Guangxu Emperor**. The two argued, though, and Cixi had Guangxu thrown in prison, where he later died.

Pu Yi Becomes Emperor

When he arrived in the Forbidden City, tiny Pu Yi was rushed to his great aunt's deathbed. The wizened, sickly old lady must have been an amazing and terrifying sight to the young boy. She wore a cape decorated with four thousand pearls, **jade** bracelets and rings, and tiny shoes trimmed with pearls and jade. Cixi told Pu Yi that he was to be the next emperor of China and she gave him the **reign name** of Xuantong, which means "Ceremony of Tribute." From that day on, nothing in Pu Yi's life would ever be the same again. Cixi died the next day and was buried wearing her jewels.

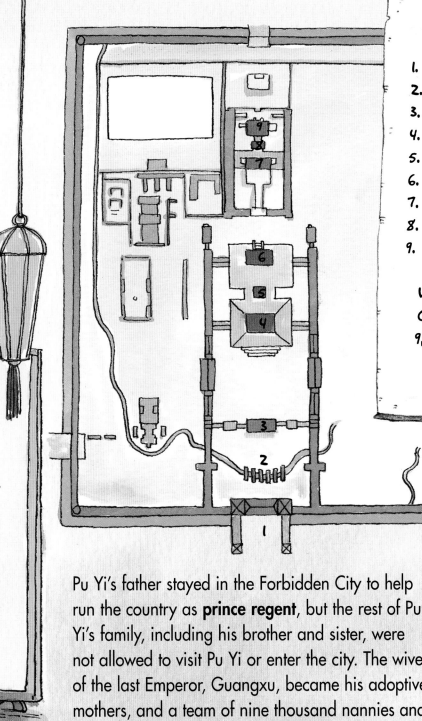

Plan of the forbidden City

1. Meridian Gate
2. River of Golden Water
3. Gate of Supreme Harmony
4. Hall of Supreme Harmony
5. Hall of Perfect Harmony
6. Hall of Preserving Harmony
7. Palace of Heavenly Purity
8. Palace of Earthly Tranquillity
9. Gate of Divine Military Genius

Within the walls of the city was a complex of glittering palaces with 9,999 rooms (9 is a lucky number for the Chinese), filled with fabulous treasures!

JADE

Jade is prized by the Chinese for its warm color and amazing strength. It is the toughest of all precious stones. Jade can be broken, but never twisted out of shape, making it a symbol of honor, nobility, and constancy. Jade ornaments and jewelry and statuettes were worn by officials in the Forbidden City to show how important they were.

Pu Yi's father stayed in the Forbidden City to help run the country as **prince regent**, but the rest of Pu Yi's family, including his brother and sister, were not allowed to visit Pu Yi or enter the city. The wives of the last Emperor, Guangxu, became his adoptive mothers, and a team of nine thousand nannies and special servants tried to provide Pu Yi with everything he needed. He was not allowed to play with other children or leave his new home and he spent his days surrounded by adults who treated him as a living god.

Life in the forbidden city

Everywhere Pu Yi went he was followed by crowds of servants carrying food, medicine, and clothing in case the little emperor wanted anything. Every imaginable entertainment was provided for him. He was taught how to fly kites and he learned martial arts. He could even summon orchestras to play for him with just the snap of his fingers. Pu Yi liked to ride around on a bicycle and through special gaps that were cut into the walls in the palace grounds so he could ride where he pleased. Sometimes the spoiled young emperor would tire of the constant attention and would take out his frustration on other people, ordering men to be beaten for his entertainment.

CHINESE OPERA

Music and song had been popular in China since the 7th century. Eventually Chinese opera developed. All the actors were male, dressing up as women to play the female roles. The characters in Chinese opera were divided up into four types—Sheng (emperors, generals, gentlemen), Qing (villains, rebels, outlaws), Dan (females) and Chou (comedy characters).

12

KUNG FU

Martial arts, such as **kung fu**, first appeared in China thousands of years ago. They were practiced by **Shaolin monks**, who believed that a strong body would help them keep a strong mind. Many of the techniques are based on the movements of animals such as the tiger and eagle.

A day in my life as Emperor by Pu Yi *

9am   Got up early and ate breakfast.

10am Played chess and I won easily. No one here seems to be able to beat me.

11am Competitive poetry reading against the head eunuch. I win again!

12pm Painted a picture of my beautiful palace.

1pm   Lunch served exactly when I want.

2pm   Played my favorite game, hide and seek. The eunuchs can never find me!

3pm   Fishing, caught lots of colorful carp.

4pm   Cricket fighting, excellent! My pet cricket is really tough, a real champion!

5pm   Chinese opera. Started off well, but got a bit boring. Nodded off halfway through.

9pm   Fireworks, great! Lots of noise and color!

* This is how Pu Yi might have described his day, in his diary!

In 1911, when Pu Yi was just five years old, the Qing Dynasty collapsed. The people grew tired of their Imperial Manchu leaders. A group of **revolutionaries**, led by **Dr. Sun Yat-sen**, took over the Chinese government. China was declared a **Republic**, which meant all future leaders would have to be elected by the people. More than 2,000 years of monarchy would come to an end, and there would no longer be an emperor. Pu Yi was forced to give up his throne. A deal was struck with the new government allowing the young emperor to continue living in the Forbidden City, enjoying the same privileges as he had before.

The Emperor's Clothes

Everybody in the Forbidden City had to dress and wear their hair in the same way. The men grew their hair long in the back and wore it in a long braid called a **queue**. The Manchu people thought very highly of horses and the queue was designed to look like a horse's tail. The women wore their hair coiled on the tops of their heads. Clothes were made from silk or cotton and were decorated with mythical animals, believed to protect the wearer from harm and bring them good fortune. The Chinese had produced silk for over 2,000 years, spinning this valuable material that came from silkworms. Silk was in great demand both in China and in other countries and exporting it had helped China become rich.

Fans were an extremely popular fashion accessory in China. They originally came from Japan and soon became a status symbol. The rich always made sure they had the right fan for the right season. You could even write or paint on someone else's fan as a sign of true friendship.

As emperor, Pu Yi had special privileges. He wore a pattern of a ferocious five-clawed dragon on his clothes and sometimes he would wear shoes with high heels to make him taller than less important people, and keep him away from the dirty ground. But most importantly, he was the only person in the Forbidden City who was allowed to wear yellow. Everything Pu Yi had was yellow; his sedan chair, the bridle for his horse, the dishes and plates he ate from, even his pillowcase!

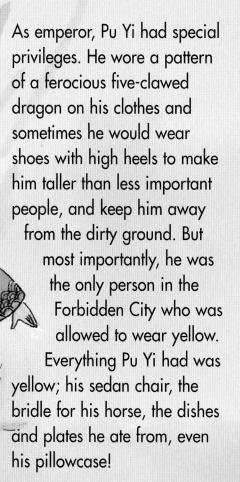

My Brother's Visit *

Today my mother brought my brother and sister to visit me in the Forbidden City. We had not seen each other for four years and I was thrilled to be with them again. We played hide and seek in the grounds of the palace, but in the middle of our game, I suddenly noticed the color of my brother's sleeves. They were yellow! I was furious and flew into a great rage! My brother was terrified of me and tried to explain that the sleeves of his jacket were peach, not yellow. However, I was not convinced, and made my brother bow down before me and ask for my forgiveness. No one but the emperor should ever wear imperial yellow, not even the emperor's brother!

* When Pu Yi and his brother argued, this is how Pu Yi might have described the event.

FASHIONABLE FEET

Beauty was a painful business for women in Imperial China. Small feet were considered very elegant and young girls had their feet tightly bound to stop them from growing. This turned the feet into a kind of gnarled hooves, which were agony to walk on. Poets of the time loved the look, though, describing such feet as "golden lilies." Foot binding only stopped about a hundred years ago.

Food and Drink

Meals were great occasions in the Forbidden City. Every day up to twenty five different dishes were prepared for Pu Yi, cooked by many chefs. They had to be ready to serve food at a moment's notice, day or night, whenever the emperor ordered "Transmit the viands!" (bring me the food!) Pu Yi might have ten different courses for breakfast, followed by up to twenty different courses for lunch, just a few hours later! The incredible quantities of food would be laid out on six tables in front of the emperor. Two would hold main dishes of meat and fish, one would hold vegetables, while the remainder would be overflowing with rice and cakes.

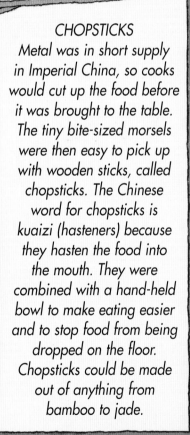

CHOPSTICKS
Metal was in short supply in Imperial China, so cooks would cut up the food before it was brought to the table. The tiny bite-sized morsels were then easy to pick up with wooden sticks, called chopsticks. The Chinese word for chopsticks is kuaizi (hasteners) because they hasten the food into the mouth. They were combined with a hand-held bowl to make eating easier and to stop food from being dropped on the floor. Chopsticks could be made out of anything from bamboo to jade.

Monthly shopping list
for the Forbidden City *

5000 chickens
3000 ducks
10 tons of pork
1000 cakes
3000 lychee fruits
2000 water chestnuts
2000 bottles of wine
1000 fish
3000 shrimp
5000 eggs
2000 bitter melons
20 tons of rice
20 tons of wheat and millet (to be
ground into flour to make noodles)
20 tons of cha (tea)

* This is what the monthly shopping list might
have looked like!

Past emperors had even bigger appetites. Pu Yi's great aunt, the Dowager Empress Cixi, chose from up to 150 different dishes every day, drank wine from a jade cup, and ate her food using golden chopsticks! Because poisoning was often used as a way of removing one's enemies, before Pu Yi began to eat, every dish was tasted by a servant, to check that it had not been poisoned.

AN IMPORTANT CROP

Along with tea, rice is one of the most important crops in China. It is vital to the country because it grows quickly enough to feed the enormous population. The Chinese lifted water into fields to create the flooded conditions that are ideal for rice growing.

School Days

As emperor, Pu Yi was given the best education that money could buy. The Imperial Palace had a special study room where the young emperor attended school. All his lessons were taught in Chinese and Manchu. Some people in the Forbidden City still hoped to return Pu Yi to power. They believed this would be easier if he had contacts in powerful Western countries, such as England and the United States of America. So when Pu Yi was thirteen, an officer from the **English Colonial Office** was appointed as PuYi's English tutor. His name was **Reginald Johnston**, and he had a great influence on the young emperor. Officially, his role was to teach the boy English, but he also acted as a link between Pu Yi and the English government.

THE INVENTION OF PAPER

*Paper as we know it was invented in 105 A.D. by **Cai Lun**, a Chinese court official. He mixed mulberry bark, hemp, and rags with water, mashed it into a pulp, pressed out the pulp into a thin layer and left it to dry in the sun. Papermakers would hang the sheets of paper on special racks to dry. The invention of paper helped literature and the arts to flourish in China.*

Johnston introduced Pu Yi to Western customs and modern technology, and gave him an English name, Henry. Pu Yi often used his Western name throughout the rest of his life. Johnston grew very fond of Pu Yi, and worried about his life in the Forbidden City. He remarked that "although he is an emperor, he is also a boy… badly in need of a change of air and surroundings." One day, when they were in class, Johnston noticed that Pu Yi seemed to have trouble reading the clock on his desk. He realized that the emperor needed glasses, so Johnston had some made for him. Officials in the Forbidden City were furious, thinking that they made the emperor look too European, but Pu Yi took no notice. He wore glasses until the day he died.

School Schedule *

9am Start school. Mr. Johnston takes attendance, but this doesn't take long, as I am the only pupil!

9.05am Poetry class. I love poetry, and write about my beautiful surroundings. I have even had some of my poems published. My pen name is "Luminous Unicorn."

10am Classics. Learning about my ancestors.

11am Calligraphy and drawing. My favorite lesson. Mr. Johnston gave me a gold star today.

12pm Quick lunch break. Just twenty courses, then back to work!

2pm Started learning English with Mr. Johnston. Great fun. I would love to travel to Europe with him one day.

* This is what Pu Yi's school schedule might have looked like.

CHINESE WRITING

Chinese writing is one of the oldest forms of writing in the world. The earliest examples date back to around 1200 B.C.. These are the so-called Oracle Bone inscriptions, which were found at the site of the last Shang capital near present-day Anyang, Henan province.

In 1899, a Peking scholar was prescribed a remedy containing 'dragon bones'. (At that time, the dragon bones usually referred to fossils of dead animals.) The scholar noticed that there was a strange form of writing on the bones he had been given at his pharmacy. This find led to the discovery of Anyang, the last capital of Shang dynasty, where archeologists have discovered a huge amount of these carved bones.

In 221 B.C. the First Emperor of Qin introduced the Qin script as the official writing of China. There are thousands of different Chinese characters, but many are ancient words that are no longer used. To be able to read Chinese today, you would need to learn about 5,000 different characters.

Pu Yi Gets Married

When Pu Yi was still a teenager, court advisors began putting pressure on him to get married. They still wanted to restore him to the throne, and believed it would help if there was an **empress** to reign beside him. Pu Yi's advisors brought him photographs of suitable Manchu girls, and asked him to pick his favorite. The pictures were poor quality, though. His first choice, a girl named **Wen Xui**, was decided to be too ugly to be empress. His second choice, a beautiful girl named **Wan Rong** (who later took the Western name of Elizabeth) became his official wife and empress, while Wen Xui became his consort (a kind of unofficial second wife).

Would like to meet... *

* Hello, my great emperor. My name is Wen Xui and I originally came from Manchuria. I have silky dark hair that I tie on top of my head in the style of the Manchus. I love horseback riding and kite flying. I have dreamed of serving your greatness since I was a little girl.

* Greetings, my emperor. My name is Wan Rong and I am hoping to be your wife. I love writing poetry, going to the opera, and playing chess. I have always wanted to live in the Forbidden City, ever since I first saw your photo.

* Pu Yi's future brides may have written letters to him like these!

Getting married in China was a complicated business. Once a suitable girl was found, a **matchmaker** made the wedding proposal. If it was accepted, the couple's birthdays were checked to make sure they were compatible according to **astrology**. Next, a betrothal letter was written to make the engagement official, and then a gift letter was handed over, listing the presents the groom's family would like to be given by the bride's family. The next step was the giving of betrothal gifts and then wedding gifts. A wedding date was chosen, once again using astrology. Finally the wedding ceremony took place. On the wedding morning, the bride took a bath in grapefruit juice, put on a red dress, and rode in a sedan chair to meet the bridegroom. The wedding would be sealed with a wedding letter, confirming the formal acceptance of the bride into the groom's family.

The Modern Emperor

At the age of sixteen, Pu Yi made an attempt to escape the Forbidden City by bribing the Imperial guards. However, they took his money then betrayed him, and he never made it past the huge stone lions that stood at the palace gates. Outside the walls of the city the political situation in China was still uncertain. Some people wanted to restore the monarchy. Others supported the republic. A third group was in favor of a new political movement, called **communism**. In 1924, a communist Chinese warlord and a bitter enemy of the Manchus, **Feng Yuxiang**, stormed the Forbidden City. Pu Yi was forced to leave the palace for good. Carrying just a suitcase full of jewels, he stepped outside the towering walls. He was now an ordinary man.

OPIUM

Many people in China were addicted to a drug called opium, including Pu Yi's wife, Elizabeth. Opium was made from poppy seeds and had been used in China for hundreds of years as a painkiller. When people began to mix it with tobacco, opium addiction became a huge problem for the country.

Tianjin Society Gossip Column *

* The former emperor and his radiant wife, Elizabeth, have been spotted shopping. Elizabeth bought three expensive silk dresses, while Pu Yi decided on a diamond tie pin and a carved walking stick.

* The famous Chinese opera actor Mei Lan-fang was introduced to Pu Yi and his beautiful wife Elizabeth at a party held at the Tianjin country club.

* Scandal at Chang Garden. We hear that Pu Yi booked an orchestra to play for his wife's birthday but then suddenly canceled. It is rumored that officials warned Pu Yi that this Western display of wealth was not suitable for a former emperor of China.

* A newspaper column like this may have existed in Pu Yi's day.

Pu Yi and his family fled first to the Japanese **Embassy** and then to the Japanese-controlled city of **Tianjin**, where Pu Yi had supporters. There, Pu Yi and his wives enjoyed a busy social life, meeting people from all over the world. They stayed in Chang Garden, a large, modern house with a flushing toilet and central heating, which were unusual for the time. Dressed in Western-style clothes, Pu Yi mixed with poets, doctors, writers, astrologers, and even sports stars and he lavished gifts on the warlords and supporters he believed might one day help him return to the throne. In private, though, Pu Yi's marriage to Elizabeth was unhappy, and his other wife, Wen Xui, jealous at always being second choice, asked for a divorce. When Chinese revolutionaries looted his ancestors' tombs in 1928, Pu Yi's happiness was shattered and his hatred of the Chinese grew stronger.

THE DESIGNER EMPEROR
Pu Yi spent his money at an amazing rate, filling Chang Garden with modern luxuries such as pianos, clocks, and radios. He wore leather shoes, a wrist watch, and diamond cufflinks, and bought designer glasses from Germany.

The Puppet Emperor

In 1931, the Japanese army invaded Manchuria. The ongoing **Civil War** in China meant the political situation was chaotic and although Manchuria was now a part of China, the Japanese were able to take control of the region. The Japanese set up a new country called **Manchukuo**. In 1932, they tried to tempt Pu Yi back from Tianjin, as a possible leader, offering to smuggle him into the country he had left years before. Pu Yi eagerly accepted, thinking he would be an emperor once again, and wanting to help anyone take power from the Chinese. He was to be bitterly disappointed. His new role was simply as a puppet emperor, a powerless figurehead for the new country. All the important decisions were made by the Japanese. They read all his mail and only permitted him to talk to his closest relations.

CHINESE RELIGION

Throughout history a number of different religions or philosophies (teachings) have been followed in China. Confucianism follows the teachings of the philosopher Confucius. He believed that people should live by precise rules—if each person knows his place in the family, then ultimately each village and city will become perfect. Daoism is another philosophy that preaches harmony in all things, uniting opposites such as negative and positive, earth and sky.

My Buddhist beliefs by Pu Yi *

Against the wishes of the Japanese, I have become a devout Buddhist. This religion came to China from India nearly two thousand years ago, and is now as popular as Confucianism and Daoism. Buddhism teaches that you can only be happy when you remove desire from your life and stop wanting things. This can be achieved through meditation. You sit silently for long periods of time with your mind totally focused on your beliefs and emptied of all other thoughts. I now believe that all life is sacred and have become a vegetarian. My servants must not swat flies and must stop my cats from killing mice.

* This is what Pu Yi might have believed.

Pu Yi was given a palace and lots of money. He was encouraged by his Japanese masters to marry into a rich Japanese family. This would ensure that they had a spy inside the family of their puppet emperor. Pu Yi resisted at first but eventually agreed to take a new wife, a Manchu girl called **Yuqin** ("Jade Lute") who had been to a Japanese school. Pu Yi was also asked to convert to the Japanese religion of **Shintoism.** Publicly he embraced his new religion but in private he rebelled against it, becoming a devout **Buddhist.**

CHINESE HOROSCOPES

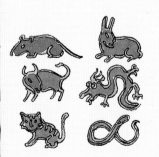

Chinese horoscopes were a key part of everyday life in Imperial China. They were used to make decisions about issues such as marriage. The horoscope is made up of a cycle of 12 animals that each have certain years dedicated to them: the Rat, Ox, Tiger, Rabbit, Dragon, Snake, Horse, Sheep, Monkey, Rooster, Dog, and Pig. The year you were born determined which animal ruled you and was thought to affect how your life would turn out.

The Prisoner Emperor

Pu Yi continued his protected but pointless life as emperor of Manchukuo. During the Second World War, though, Manchukuo was used as a base by Japan. When the war ended, Manchukuo was invaded by the **Soviets**. Pu Yi was arrested and flown to the **USSR**. He left his wives behind and never saw them again. Because the Soviet authorities thought he might be useful, Pu Yi was treated very well. He was an important witness for the Soviets and their **Western allies** against the Japanese. Pu Yi testified against the Japanese war criminals who had once been his supporters. Eventually Pu Yi was sent back to China. Once there, he was immediately thrown into a prison camp, because Chinese authorities considered him a traitor.

My daily prison routine by Pu Yi *

7am	Breakfast of pickled vegetables, porridge, salted eggs, and rice.
8am	Cleaning cells and folding clothes.
12pm	Gardening and digging the vegetable patch.
2pm	Lunch. I handed out food to fellow prisoners.
3pm	Made boxes for packing pencils in.
4pm	Reading time, started Mao's "Little Red Book."
6pm	Dinner. Rice and chicken again!
7pm	Confession to authorities. I promised to be more like Chairman Mao and have memorized some sayings from the "Little Red Book."
8pm	Started writing my autobiography!
11pm	Lights out.

* This is what Pu Yi's prison routine might have been like.

In the Chinese prison camp, the prison guards who had once been his subjects laughed and mocked Pu Yi. They ridiculed his Buddhist beliefs, forcing him to kill mice and flies against his will. Sleeping in a cell with other prisoners, the spoiled former emperor was forced to learn skills that he had never had to master before—simple things such as tying his shoelaces and brushing his teeth. Eventually, Pu Yi was sent to work in the prison gardens. There he developed a love of nature. Working outdoors by himself gave him the sort of freedom he had never known inside the claustrophobic walls of the Forbidden City.

THE PEOPLE'S REPUBLIC OF CHINA

When the Republic failed to improve the lives of the Chinese people, the communist movement grew more and more popular. After World War II, the communists forced the republicans out of China and proclaimed the creation of the **People's Republic of China**. The wealthy were forced to give up their land for the common good. This did not work. Millions of Chinese people starved to death. **Chairman Mao** was one of the founding members of the **Chinese Communist Party (CCP)**. His "Little Red Book" was a handbook designed to help fellow communists live in the right way and stay on the right path. Citizens had to carry a copy with them at all times.

Return to the forbidden city

In 1959, a far more practical Pu Yi was finally released from prison. The communist party considered him reformed and no longer a traitor, and he was issued a special pardon by Chairman Mao. The harsh experience had taught him many valuable skills. Pu Yi now began life as an ordinary Chinese citizen. The government sent him to the Botanical Gardens in the capital city Beijing, where he combined jobs for the government with work as a gardener and handyman. He lived in a dilapidated house close to the Forbidden City and lovingly tended a small plot of ground that was just a tiny fraction of what he had once owned.

Soon after his release from prison, Pu Yi was introduced to a nurse called **Shuxian**. They were married in 1962. He was madly in love, and told his wife that, "I have nothing in this world except you. You are my life." Pu Yi's old home, the Forbidden City, was now open to the public. As an ordinary citizen, he had to wait in line to buy a ticket when he wanted to visit the palaces where he had once lived in such splendor. Despite being poor and having to work, Pu Yi now enjoyed genuine happiness for the first time in his life. That happiness would end when Pu Yi, the last emperor of China, died of cancer in 1967.

My day trip to the Forbidden City by Pu Yi *

Today I visited my old home and I rode on a bus. It's a much more interesting way to travel than being carried in a sedan chair! I visited the Gate of Heavenly Peace and then went into the palace. The decorations have been changed and everything has been repainted. There are new carpets and curtains everywhere. The Palace Museum is no longer filled with jade and porcelain. Instead it is now a factory, producing tablecloths and curtains. I walked through the Imperial Garden that had seemed such a lonely place to me. I was filled with joy to see the garden alive with young children, playing and laughing.

* This is what Pu Yi might have written about his visit.

THE CULTURAL REVOLUTION

In 1966, Mao started a program called the Cultural Revolution. This was a war on the culture of old China: old ideas, old customs, and old habits. The Red Guards attacked and destroyed treasures such as temples, books, and works of art. They also attacked anyone who they believed did not agree with the revolution. The prisons were full of prisoners, many of whom died either from beatings or from lack of medical care. The revolution lasted for nearly three years.

29

Glossary

ASTROLOGY The study of the planets and how they influence people's lives and personalities.

BEIJING The capital city of China.

BUDDHIST A person who follows Buddhism, a religion that teaches happiness can only be achieved in life when you stop wanting things.

CAI LUN The inventor of paper.

CHARACTERS The letters and words that are used in Chinese writing.

CHINA A large country in Asia.

CHINESE COMMUNIST PARTY A political party formed in China after World War II.

CIVIL WAR A war between two or more groups within the same country.

CIXI (DOWAGER EMPRESS) The ruler of China 1862–1908 and Pu Yi's great aunt.

COMMUNISM A system in which the government owns all property and there is only one political party.

DOWAGER EMPRESS A woman (normally elderly) who became the ruler of China when her husband, the emperor, died. She would rule from behind the scenes, as women were not allowed to rule directly.

DYNASTIES Powerful families who ruled China for years at a time.

EMBASSY A country's official building in a foreign country, where their Ambassador and other officials live and work.

EMPEROR The ruler of China.

EMPRESS A female ruler of China, or the wife of the Emperor.

ENGLISH COLONIAL OFFICE The part of the British Government that controlled Britain's trade routes and sea ports in China and the British-ruled colony of Hong Kong.

FENG YUXIANG A communist Chinese warlord.

FORBIDDEN CITY A walled complex of palaces in Beijing. The home of the Chinese emperors.

GUANGXU EMPEROR The ruler of China 1875–1908 and Pu Yi's uncle.

IMPERIAL Another way to describe something or someone royal.

IMPERIAL CHINA China during the period when it was ruled by an imperial (royal) family.

JADE A green precious stone.

JOHNSTON, REGINALD Pu Yi's English tutor.

KUNG FU A popular Chinese martial art.

MANCHU A person from Manchuria.

MANCHUKUO The new country set up in Manchuria by the Japanese in 1932.

MANCHURIA A large country to the northeast of China. Now part of modern day China.

MAO (CHAIRMAN) One of the founding members and leader of the Chinese Communist Party (CCP).

MATCHMAKER A person who arranges marriages.

MONGOLIA A vast country to the north of China.

PEOPLE'S REPUBLIC OF CHINA The name given to China when the communists took power.

PRINCE CHUN Pu Yi's father.

PRINCE REGENT A person who rules in the absence of a king or emperor, or if a king or emperor is too young to rule on their own.

QIN SCRIPT The official writing of China introduced in 221 B.C.

QING DYNASTY Pu Yi's dynasty, the last to rule China.

QUEUE A braid worn by Manchu men.

REIGN NAME Emperors were given an official reign name. They were too important to be addressed by their personal name.

REPUBLIC A country where the leader is elected by the people, who are then able to have a say in how their country is run.

REVOLUTIONARIES People taking